RENOVATOR'S DREAM

7 INTERACTIVE BIBLE STUDIES FOR
SMALL GROUPS AND INDIVIDUALS

PHIL CAMPBELL
AND GREG CLARKE

Renovator's Dream
Second edition
© Phil Campbell and Matthias Media 2011

First published 2003

Matthias Media
(St Matthias Press Ltd ACN 067 558 365)
PO Box 225
Kingsford NSW 2032
Australia
Telephone: (02) 9663 1478; international: +61-2-9663-1478
Facsimile: (02) 9663 3265; international: +61-2-9663-3265
Email: info@matthiasmedia.com.au
Internet: www.matthiasmedia.com.au

Matthias Media (USA)
Telephone: 330 953 1702; international: +1-330-953-1702
Facsimile: 330 953 1712; international: +1-330-953-1712
Email: sales@matthiasmedia.com
Internet: www.matthiasmedia.com

ISBN 978 1 921441 94 3

Cover design and typesetting by Matthias Media.
Series concept designs by Lankshear Design Pty Ltd.

⟩⟩ CONTENTS

» HOW TO MAKE THE MOST OF THESE STUDIES

1. What is an Interactive Bible Study?

Interactive Bible Studies are a bit like a guided tour of a famous city. They take you through a particular part of the Bible, helping you to know where to start, pointing out things along the way, suggesting avenues for further exploration, and making sure that you know how to get home. Like any good tour, the real purpose is to allow you to go exploring for yourself—to dive in, have a good look around, and discover for yourself the riches that God's word has in store.

In other words, these studies aim to provide stimulation and input and point you in the right direction, while leaving you to do plenty of the exploration and discovery yourself.

We hope that these studies will stimulate lots of 'interaction'—interaction with the Bible, with the things we've written, with your own current thoughts and attitudes, with other people as you discuss them, and with God as you talk to him about it all.

2. The format

The studies contain five main components:
- sections of text that introduce, inform, summarize and challenge
- numbered questions that help you examine the passage and think through its meaning
- sidebars that provide extra bits of background or optional extra study ideas, especially regarding other relevant parts of the Bible
- 'Implications' sections that help you think about what this passage means for you and your life today
- suggestions for thanksgiving and prayer as you close.

3. How to use these studies on your own

- Before you begin, pray that God would open your eyes to what he is saying in the Bible, and give you the spiritual strength to do something about it.
- Work through the study, reading the text, answering the questions about the Bible passage, and exploring the sidebars as you have time.
- Resist the temptation to skip over the 'Implications' and 'Give thanks and pray' sections at the end. It is important that we not only hear and understand God's word, but also respond to it. These closing sections help us do that.
- Take what opportunities you can to talk to others about what you've learnt.

4. How to use these studies in a small group

- Much of the above applies to group study as well. The studies are suitable for structured Bible study or cell groups, as well as for more informal pairs and triplets. Get together with a friend or friends and work through them at your own pace; use them as the basis for regular Bible study with your spouse. You don't need the formal structure of a 'group' to gain maximum benefit.

- For small groups, it is *very useful* if group members can work through the study themselves *before* the group meets. The group discussion can take place comfortably in an hour (depending on how sidetracked you get!) if all the members have done some work in advance.
- The role of the group leader is to direct the course of the discussion and to try to draw the threads together at the end. If you are a group leader, the material in the appendix 'Tips for leaders' will help you think through how to use these studies in a group setting.
- If your group members usually don't work through the study in advance, it's extra important that the leader prepares which parts to concentrate on, and which parts to glide past more quickly. In particular, the leader will need to select which of the 'Implications' to focus on.
- We haven't included an 'answer guide' to the questions in the studies. This is a deliberate move. We want to give you a guided tour of the Bible, not a lecture. There is more than enough in the text we have written and the questions we have asked to point you in what we think is the right direction. The rest is up to you.

5. Bible translation

Previous studies in our Interactive Bible Study series have assumed that most readers would be using the New International Version of the Bible. However, since the release of the English Standard Version in 2001, many have switched to the ESV for study purposes. For this reason, we have decided to quote from and refer to the ESV text, which we recommend.

THE PROMISE KEEPER

[NEHEMIAH 1-2]

1. Have you ever made any New Year's resolutions that you didn't keep? What went wrong?

ATTENTION HOUSE BUILDERS, CEOs and personnel managers! Apparently, Nehemiah is the book for you. This Old Testament account of the rebuilding of part of Jerusalem has been variously labelled as a builder's manual, a handbook on management and a how-to guide for getting your employees to do their jobs.

But is it about any of these things?

As you might expect, there is a grain of truth in each of these approaches to Nehemiah. It is certainly about building walls—but not just any backyard fence. These are the very significant walls of Israel's holiest city. And yes, there's plenty in the book about Nehemiah the leader, the man who convinced a foreign king to let him return from exile to restore his forefathers' home. But to use this book as a company handbook would be to miss the point.

Nehemiah is, in fact, the diary of a disaster. It's the account of the many successes—but larger failure—of one leader in restoring holy living among his people. It's the story of how bricks and mortar just aren't enough to rebuild a nation's heart. It's the account of how Israel, God's chosen people, remained in need of a saviour at the close of what we call the Old Testament.

Nehemiah brings the biblical record of Israel's rise and fall to a close—it is the last historical Bible book before the time of Jesus. It records how Nehemiah left his position as a high official in the court of the Persian king to return to Israel to rebuild the city walls. It tells of how those Jews who returned from exile also turned away from their sins and recommitted themselves to the Law of Moses. But, tragically, it also reveals their return to old sinful ways—the ways that had brought God's judgement upon their forefathers.

As we approach this book, let's look back to the beginning of God's relationship with Israel.

Read Genesis 12:1–7.

2. What does God promise to do for Abram's descendants, and for the whole world?

Read Deuteronomy 29:22–30:6.

3. As Israel is about to enter the Promised Land, what warning does God give?

4. What promise does God make?

ISRAEL WAS GIVEN VERY CLEAR instructions about how to live in the Promised Land. God couldn't have made it plainer. At the same time that he made the promises, God revealed to Israel that they wouldn't be able to keep his word— they would fall short and turn against him. But even then, God promised that he would 'restore their fortunes' if they turned back to him with all their heart and soul. This pattern of instruction, sin, repentance and restoration would occur time and again in Israel's history.

So at the point where Nehemiah begins, what is the state of God's relationship with Israel?

Read Nehemiah 1.

5. What is the situation for Israel and for Nehemiah as he writes?

6. Nehemiah is written in the style of a diary. What do we learn here in chapter 1 about Nehemiah, the man?

7. Summarize Nehemiah's request to God.

8. Nehemiah remembers some of God's earlier promises. What were they (Lev 26:33; Deut 30:4; 1 Kgs 8:48-49)?

9. What is the required starting point for Israel's renewed relationship with God (v. 9)?

First the good news

NEHEMIAH'S CONFIDENCE COMES from his understanding of God's promises. When God makes a promise, he keeps it through years and generations. When you know what God has promised in his word, you can be sure that it will come about. This is good news when the promise is that he will keep his "steadfast love with those who love him and keep his commandments" (1:5)—but bad news when Israel hasn't kept its side of the bargain.

Nehemiah sets about to bring Israel back to God.

Read Nehemiah 2.

10. What does Nehemiah want to do, and why?

11. Why does the king grant his requests?

12. What are Sanballat and Tobiah worried about (v. 10)? How do they react to Nehemiah's plan (v. 19)?

Make a mental note to watch these two characters through the rest of the book.

13. Why is Nehemiah confident that he will succeed (vv. 18, 20)?

» Implications

- Why can Nehemiah say that those opposing him "have no portion or right or claim in Jerusalem"? (1:20)

- There is a conflict between authorities in this chapter. In what ways do you feel threatened by authorities other than God himself? In what areas do you find it difficult to maintain a commitment to "the God of heaven" above all others?

- Do you feel that God will keep his promises? Why/why not?

- In what ways does Nehemiah's prayer demonstrate his good grasp of God's character? How can such knowledge help us in our prayers?

» Give thanks and pray

- Thank God for being "the great and awesome God who keeps covenant and steadfast love with those who love him and keep his commandments".
- Ask God to help you trust that he is in control of the whole world, including people who jeer and despise God and his people.
- Pray for yourself and for Christians in your church and all over the world, keeping in mind the great example of Nehemiah in chapter 1, that you would be prayerful servants who delight in the fear of the Lord.

>> STUDY 2

GOD THE BUILDER

[NEHEMIAH 3-4]

1. Have you ever experienced opposition to Christian activities? How did you respond?

Building approval and opposition

THERE ARE PLENTY OF JOKES ABOUT how difficult it is to get a building project done—councils turn building plans into political issues, neighbours complain, and it just seems hard to get a decent plumber when you need one. Nothing much seems to have changed since the time when Nehemiah was trying to rebuild the walls around Jerusalem.

In the last study, we heard of how Nehemiah's attempts to keep his rebuilding plans secret failed, and a handful of Jew-haters started to oppose his work. Here in chapter 3, he pushes forward regardless, with the help of a roll call of Jews who have returned to Jerusalem from exile. But he is going to face increasing conflict with Israel's enemies before the job is done.

As you skim through chapter 3, imagine you are on a tour around Jerusalem, moving from the Sheep Gate, past the towers and around the various other gates (spare a thought for the builders at the Dung Gate).

Quickly read Nehemiah 3.

2. Note down some of the details about who builds what.

3. How would you describe the general attitude of the builders?

4. Is there anyone who refuses to participate? What might this suggest?

5. How does this record of names and deeds help us to understand the significance of what was happening?

6. Does this strike you as genuine history or national myth? What features affect your conclusions?

THE UNITY AND EFFECTIVENESS OF the wall rebuilders is impressive. They seem to be strongly motivated to repair their city, with the notable exception of the Tekoite nobles (3:5). All manner of Jews seem to be involved, from rulers and priests, to sons and daughters, to tradespeople, perfumers and goldsmiths. It is a picture of a national group cooperating for the greater good. If only Israel had always acted like this!

Chapter 3 is a summary of the work that took place; chapters 4-6 let us in on some of the drama that accompanied this work.

Read Nehemiah 4.

7. How would you describe Sanballat's and Tobiah's reactions to the building of the wall?

8. Is Nehemiah's prayer in verses 4-5 reasonable? Why/why not?

9. What two threats emerge to hamper the completion of the wall (v. 8)?

10. How do the Israelites gather their strength (vv. 9, 14)?

11. This is not the first time a leader of Israel has told his people to "not be afraid" and to "remember the Lord" (v. 14). What other event in Israel's history may have sprung to mind for Nehemiah's men (Deut 1:8, 29-31; 7:21-22)?

12. How would you describe the manner in which the Israelites work in verses 15-23?

13. Read Exodus 14:13-14 and Deuteronomy 1:30. Why could Nehemiah so confidently assert in verse 20 that "Our God will fight for us"? What links the events taking place around Nehemiah with the events that took place in Israel's past?

14. Read 2 Corinthians 1:19-20. All of God's promises are fulfilled in Jesus Christ. So what are we to make of the specific promises God gave to Israel— the promises to which Nehemiah keeps referring? Do they apply at all to us today? Read the following New Testament passages and answer the relevant questions (if you are short on time, just choose one of the passages).

	Galatians 3:16-22	Romans 4:13-25	Hebrews 8:6-13
What is said about the old promises (or old covenant)?			
What is said about the new promises (or new covenant)?			
In what sense do the promises to Abraham or Moses mentioned in the passage apply to Christians?			
In what sense do the promises to Abraham or Moses mentioned in the passage *not* apply to Christians?			

God's work

IT IS PROFOUNDLY TRUE THAT THE rebuilding of Jerusalem's walls was a work of God. In the face of strong opposition—taunts, provocation and physical attacks—the Israelites managed not only to construct the wall, but to fight off the enemy at the same time. In one hand was the hammer; in the other was the sword. It is an image that might swell a leader's pride.

However, the Jews can take little credit for their work. Nehemiah makes it clear that God has been behind them, protecting them, fighting for them, remaining faithful to his promises to them. Without God 'on their side', Jerusalem would have been lost once more.

It is important that we understand this national pride properly. Israel should not glory in its status; rather, it is humbled by God's love and commitment to his people. He has taken a ragged bunch of exiles, a conquered mob, and through them rebuilt their home. Israel is to remember their "great and awesome" Lord, and remember that they only triumph by his power and love.

» Implications

- A friend says to you, "Our church is undertaking a building project in the spirit of Nehemiah. We are trusting God to protect us from any opposition, and to provide for all of our needs." What, if anything, is wrong with this present-day application of Nehemiah's account?

- Is it right or wrong to pray that God will bring his enemies to justice?

- Are you one of God's enemies or do you seek for his name to be honoured?

- In times of hardship, how does remembering the Lord help us to face opposition? What exactly do you remember about the Lord in order to gain courage and strength?

» Give thanks and pray

- Thank God for fulfilling all his promises in Jesus Christ.
- Pray that you would learn from Israel's mistakes and remain steadfast in your faith in Christ, remembering him as your only salvation.
- Ask God to help you not to be afraid but to remember to rely on him next time you face opposition in his name.

LEADING BY EXAMPLE

[NEHEMIAH 5]

1. Should a person always take all that he or she is entitled to? Why, or why not?

Justice for all?

Which family has never heard the words "It's not fair!" issuing from the mouths of its members? It is one of the most common human complaints, and it seems to be particularly acute in families. When we see one of 'our own' suffering, or one elevated a long way above the rest, it sets our injustice bells ringing. Why should one be in luxury while another struggles to survive?

After the wall has been built, Nehemiah encounters just such a complaint from some of the Jews. They have been impoverished by a famine and sunk into debt and slavery. Perhaps the building of the wall had taken an undue economic toll on these more vulnerable citizens. Nehemiah faces a question of social justice for his new city. Where will he turn to sort things out?

Read Nehemiah 5:1–9.

2. List the kinds of problems that some of the Jews were facing.

3. List the kinds of wicked activities in which the nobles and officials were engaged.

4. What specifically was wrong with this situation (Exod 22:25; Lev 25:35-46)? What does it reveal about the way in which they intended to honour God's law?

5. What was Nehemiah's fear (v. 9)?

6. What do you think was Nehemiah's *greatest* fear? As returned exiles, what were the nobles and officials putting at risk by their behaviour (Deut 30:1-6, 15-18)?

Power corrupts

THERE ARE PERILS TO BEING A leader. Many of us know that power corrupts, either because we have been on the receiving end or because we have been the ones corrupted. At the very least, many of us will know the temptations that even just a little power brings to the dark human heart. These perils and temptations have got the better of the nobles and officials in renovated Jerusalem. They are feathering their own nests. They are keeping their own flesh and blood in slavery. They are committing the sin of usury—charging interest of their disadvantaged fellow Israelites. Angered, Nehemiah pondered what Israel was doing: they were directly violating the Law of Moses. They were breaking covenant with their God yet again, just as they did before the Exile—and Nehemiah was well aware of the consequences of such disobedience.

As well as committing wrong, the Jews were failing to do what is right. They weren't caring for the downtrodden; they weren't feeding the hungry; they weren't redeeming Jewish slaves; they didn't fear the Lord and his ways. And, as Jesus would warn his disciples, when you do not care for a brother in need, you do not care for your God (Matt 25:31-46).

Nehemiah calls Israel to repent, and Israel's reaction is instructive.

Read Nehemiah 5:9-19.

7. How did the nobles and officials respond to Nehemiah's orders (vv. 9-13)?

8. What is the significance of Nehemiah not making use of "the food allowance of the governor"? (See 1 Kings 4:22-23 for how different this allowance was from Solomon's.)

9. What is Nehemiah's motivation for acting humbly and generously (v. 15)?

CLEARLY, NEHEMIAH SETS AN example here that any leader would be wise to emulate. He responds to cries for help. He seeks to do justice, as well as making amends for the damage done. He is righteously angry about the wickedness he sees, but he reacts thoughtfully and judiciously (vv. 6-7). He gives clear directions to others, and they obey his lead. And he denies himself the spoils of leadership, instead opting to identify with the people whom he serves.

Nehemiah's motivation is intriguing. Did he lead in order to establish a great nation? No, not primarily. We are told that he led the way he did because of his fear of the Lord. His motivation was to serve God, not to displease God, and to reap God's blessings rather than his judgement. "Fear God and keep his commandments, for this is the whole duty of man", wrote another of Jerusalem's leaders (Eccl 12:13).

It remains to be seen whether Nehemiah can do a better job of inspiring the people of Israel whom he leads than did Solomon before him.

» Implications

(Choose one or more of the following to think about further or to discuss in your group.)

• Nehemiah 5 closes with an appeal to God. Similar appeals are made in Nehemiah 13:14, 22 and 31. Which of the following best paraphrases what Nehemiah seems to be praying here?

a) Reward me, God, because I have turned your people around.

b) Count up all my good deeds, God, because there are plenty of them.

c) I think I have done good deeds, God, even if everyone else has let you down.

We will come back to this question later in our studies.

• Nehemiah's actions seem to have a profound effect on those around him. In what ways have you noticed the actions of Christian leaders affecting people's confidence in God?

- Read Philippians 2:5-11. Like Nehemiah, Jesus identified himself as a 'servant king'.

  - In what ways does Jesus' service differ from Nehemiah's?

  - In what ways is it similar?

- Read 1 Peter 5:1-11. Note the ways in which Christ has provided a model for Christian leadership.

- All Christians can be tempted to fall into the sins of the Jerusalem officials. Think about ways in which you are tempted to exploit others for your own gain. You may need to pray in repentance.

- How can we gain courage from the examples of Nehemiah and Jesus? What is one area in which you can improve your humble service in the fear of the Lord this week?

» Give thanks and pray

- Praise God for our humble and obedient servant king, Jesus Christ, whom he has appointed to rule the world.
- Repent and ask forgiveness for times when you have exploited others for your own gain.
- Pray that Christian leaders (both in your own church and all over the world) will follow the examples of Nehemiah and Jesus in the way that they shepherd and serve God's people.

>> STUDY 4

FEAR OF THE LORD

[NEHEMIAH 6-7]

1. Has fear of others ever stopped you from doing what you knew, as a Christian, you should do?

The troublemaker

In the last study, we looked at some of the temptations that leaders face. In Nehemiah 6, another trap is uncovered. This time, the trap is an emotional one, appealing to Nehemiah's fear for his own life. Consider the pressures that were on him: he was given guarded permission by a conquering king to rebuild his home city; he has performed the deed in record time, with obvious divine assistance; the nations around him are getting nervous as they see what he is doing; and he has already called many of the local officials to account for their corrupt behaviour.

It is no surprise to find that there are some who would do anything to see the back of this Jewish troublemaker. But will Nehemiah succumb to fear, or will he continue to fear the Lord?

Read Nehemiah 6:1–14.

2. What was the nature of the rumour that Sanballat was spreading (vv. 6–7)? Re-read Nehemiah 2:1-8 if you can't recall the political situation.

3. How does Nehemiah respond to the intimidation?

4. Shemaiah is a prophet (v. 12), but how does Nehemiah detect that his prophecy is false?

5. There are a number of possible reasons why Nehemiah refuses to hide with Shemaiah in the temple. Can you explain them by referring to the verses given below?

- Nehemiah 2:18, 20; 4:14, 20; 6:11a, 13

- Nehemiah 6:10 (hint: this has more to do with **Shemaiah** than with Nehemiah; see Jeremiah 32:2-3 and 36:5 for a comparable situation)

- Nehemiah 6:11b, Numbers 1:51; 3:10, 38; 18:7

Shemaiah

One possible reason that hiding in the temple with Shemaiah would have been a sin for Nehemiah (v. 13) is that Shemaiah may have been banned from the temple for some reason.

The fact that he was "confined to his home" (or, as the NIV puts it, "shut in at his home") may indicate that he was ill. In Leviticus 13, a person suspected of having leprosy was to be "shut up" for seven days after the priest pronounced him unclean (Lev 13:3-8, 46; cf. vv. 21, 26, 31, 33). Or he may have been confined against his will for some other reason.

Alternatively, Shemaiah may have been part of the group who were "excluded from the priesthood as unclean" because they couldn't prove they were Israelites (Neh 7:61-65; cf. 6:10, 2:19-20).

6. In what sense does Nehemiah want the Lord to "remember" Tobiah, Sanballat and the other fearmongers (v. 14)?

Nehemiah's resolve is impressive, his reasoning even more so. He continually leans on what he *knows* about God to dispel the temptations and traps that are put before him. His understanding of God's character, God's guidance and God's promises fully equips him to continue the good work he has to do. Can you find strength in his actions for your own perseverance in the face of opposition?

Roll call

There was still plenty for the Jews to fear as they neared the completion of Jerusalem's wall. For one, they were small in number (7:4), and they had a lot of territory to defend from any disgruntled outsider. Secondly, there were webs of political connection with the surrounding nations, which threatened the integrity of the new Jerusalem. And thirdly, they had barely begun to reform and reinstate the nation's religious and social way of life. We come to that in Nehemiah 8-10, but before then Nehemiah records for us exactly who it was that made up this new effort to live as God's people in God's place.

Read Nehemiah 6:15–7:73.

7. Why is it clear to the surrounding nations that this wall "had been accomplished with the help of our God" (6:16)?

8. What impact does the completion have on the surrounding nations?

9. What awkward political situation faced Nehemiah in 6:17-19 (the term is "fifth column")?

10. How does Nehemiah manage this potential challenge to his leadership? What mattered to him more than family connections (7:2)?

11. Read Ezra 1:11-2:2. What 'roll' does Nehemiah use to 'mark off' his returned exiles? (Nehemiah 7 contains a list almost identical to Ezra 2.)

12. Nehemiah 7:61-64 highlights an important issue. Why did these people need to prove their lineage?

13. What overall impact on the unfolding story of Nehemiah do all the details of chapter 7 have?

Coming home

NEHEMIAH 7 FINISHES WITH A strong sense that Israel has come home. With the city's defence completed and the inhabitants assembled, Nehemiah has achieved a remarkable work of reform. But he knows that it has been God's work, and that it is taking place for God's sake. God is jealous for his people—"I am exceedingly jealous for Jerusalem" (Zech 1:14)—and his requirements for their holiness still stand.

How will they fare in their new endeavour?

» Implications

- Nehemiah was certain that the prophecy of Shemaiah was false. How should we test people's prophecies and claims today? (See 2 Peter 1:16-21; 1 John 4:1-6.)

- In what situations do you need to ask for God's strength so that you don't give in to fear?

» Give thanks and pray

- Praise God for his guidance, character and promises. Pray that your understanding of him will be a source of strength and perseverance.
- Ask God to help you clearly identify false prophets and not to be tempted by what they preach.
- Pray for the dispersed Jewish nation of today, that these lost children of God would humbly recognise Jesus as the true Messiah.

>> STUDY 5

THE WATER GATE AFFAIR

[NEHEMIAH 8]

1. Have you ever rediscovered in the bottom of a drawer something great that you had forgotten about? How did you feel?

You don't know what you've got

MANY CHURCHES AND DENOMINATIONS have a statement of faith or a creed that is read by the congregation, out loud together and often standing, in their public meetings. These can be moving events, as we all state what we believe. There is a sense of solidarity, of kinship, and of being part of a larger whole.

But sometimes saying the creed seems pretty stale. We merely mouth the words, empty of any meaning or significance, as we go through the motions in our Sunday morning rituals. When this happens, we really have lost touch with the privilege that it is to have the knowledge of God. We get spoilt, and we consider the revelation of God's character, his law and his actions a ponderous thing rather than the astounding wealth that it is.

In Nehemiah 8, the priest Ezra reads out the Law of Moses to the assembled Israelites in the reconstructed city of Jerusalem. They stand and listen as he reads to them the history of their nation: how God made a covenant with them, how he rescued them from slavery in Egypt, and how he gave them rules to live by in order that they would please him and prosper.

They are stunned at what they hear.

It seems that many of those present had not heard the word of the Lord for a long time, possibly ever. Their solemn assembly turns to demonstrations of humility, joy and even tears. A renewed identity is being shaped, based around the law of God.

The 'church creeds' that had been locked away for years have been found to be anything but stale. Sometimes you don't know what you've got until it's gone—and you get it back.

Read Nehemiah 8:1–12.

2. What exactly is being read to the people?

3. On what day is it being read? Why is this significant (Lev 23:23-24)?

4. How do the people respond?

5. What do the Levites do (vv. 7–8)?

6. The Israelites weep when they hear God's word. Why? Could it be connected with the events of 6:17–19?

7. Why does Nehemiah say that this is not a day of mourning, but of rejoicing?

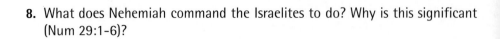

8. What does Nehemiah command the Israelites to do? Why is this significant (Num 29:1-6)?

9. Why do the people "make great rejoicing" (v. 12)?

Returning from exile, the Jews recommit themselves to the ancient ceremonies of Old Testament law. They rediscover the holy feasts and sacrifices that God has instituted through Moses, as recorded in Leviticus and Numbers.

Interestingly, the Feast of Yom Kippur, the Day of Atonement (Lev 23:27-28), is not mentioned here. It may or may not have been celebrated as part of the re-established Israel—we are not told. Nevertheless, Israel is turning away from its previous neglect of God's commands.

There is an earnest and wholehearted effort to live God's way, just as Moses had required of them in Deuteronomy 30 if they wanted God's blessing to return. And this repentance (for that's what 'turning back' is) has brought a sense of great joy.

At this point, at least, there seems to be joyous 'heart and soul' obedience from Israel. We see an instance of this glad obedience in the next section of Nehemiah 8.

Read Nehemiah 8:13-18.

10. What do the Israelites discover is supposed to happen during the feast of the seventh month (vv. 14-15)?

11. What is the festival celebrating (Lev 23:33-43, esp. v. 43)?

12. Why do they live in "booths" (or "tabernacles" [NIV] or "tents")?

13. Why is it so significant that the Israelites remember their rescue from Egypt here in Nehemiah, at this particular point in their history?

Revival

"THE LAW OF THE LORD IS PERFECT, reviving the soul", declares Psalm 19. The Israelites have experienced this revival through hearing and obeying the words read by Ezra at the Water Gate. Christians have even more reason to delight in the word of God. We have had the revelation of God's plans made clear to us in Jesus Christ, in his saving actions on the cross. We have a detailed explanation of what God has been doing in the world in the pages of our Bibles. And we have the church, the gathering of his people, within which to encourage each other, teach and rebuke each other, share the joy of the Lord, and share in our present sufferings.

Israel's experience of revival in Nehemiah 8 reminds us of what it is like to hear the word of God afresh—to wake up from a long slumber in exile and find that an abundance of guidance and blessing is ours for the taking. The elation of the Jews is almost palpable. But how do we respond to the knowledge of God that has been given us in the gospel, in Jesus and in his word?

» Implications

(Choose one or more of the following to think about further or to discuss in your group.)

• How does your reaction to the word of God compare to that of the Israelites?

• Read the celebration of the law of God in Psalm 19:7-14. Does it reflect your experience of God's word? Discuss why or why not this may be the case.

- Imagine you had not read or heard from the Bible for many years, and then you opened it up again. What do you think would strike you most?

- Do we live in a time of mourning or rejoicing? Explain your answer.

- Do you think 'festivals' of remembrance have a place for Christians today? Why/why not?

- The Levites "helped the people to understand the Law". Do we need such help today? How do we go about properly understanding God's word? You might consult the following passages while thinking about your answer: Romans 15:14-16; 1 Timothy 4:11-14; 2 Timothy 3:14-17, 4:1-6; Hebrews 1:1-2, 8:11; 1 John 2:26-27.

» Give thanks and pray

- Thank God for his kindness in revealing himself to us through his word, and for teaching us how to live.
- Ask God to give you a greater appreciation of the benefits of reading his word, and ask him to help you read it often.
- Use Psalm 19:7-14 as the basis for praise, thanks and prayer.

THE STORY OF YOUR LIFE

[NEHEMIAH 9:1–12:26]

1. If you wrote your life's story, which events, people and places would you include? Why are they significant to you?

A grand narrative

ONE OF THE MOST POPULAR activities on the internet is tracking down your ancestors. Genealogy and family history sites receive very high traffic, and their powerful search engines make tracking down that centuries-old uncle who incinerated the family mansion as easy as clicking a mouse button.

But the experience can be disappointing. Instead of finding out how your uncle ignited the kitchen when he hurled a gas lantern in a fit of rage, there's just a list of dates—born, married, deceased— and some place names where he might have lived.

The facts are there, but the story is missing.

We have a strong urge to fit the individual facts into a bigger picture. We want to find a narrative—a story with a purpose—behind the scraps and figures of history. Israel is blessed with such a record in Scripture. This nation's narrative runs back to creation itself. The reason they are in such a privileged position is that God himself has been shaping the story. Choosing Abram, God forged a history based around his own promises, character and actions.

In these last chapters of Nehemiah, this story is retold to the Israelites who have returned from exile. It provides for them their reason to live—it shapes their individual lives into the lives of 'God's people'. It is not always a pretty story. The ugly misadventures of God's people have not been censored out. Rather, we have a 'warts and all' account of how Israel stumbled and fell, and how God never failed to raise them up.

For Christian readers, this is an insight into how God works, and a very important background against which we can understand his ultimate work of salvation—including the extension of God's people among the Gentiles—in the death and resurrection of Jesus Christ.

Optional: Sackcloth and ashes

In the following passages, what do the fasting, sackcloth and ashes signify?

- 1 Samuel 7:3-6

- 2 Samuel 3:31-32

- 1 Kings 21:20-29

Read Nehemiah 9:1-5.

2. What do the actions of the Israelites in 9:1 indicate?

3. What is the significance of verse 2? Can you recall the problems caused in the past by this disobedience?

▶

4. The rest of Nehemiah 9-10 is a long speech by the Levites and a response by the people. It contains a potted history of Israel, from creation, through the exodus from Egypt, to the heights of Solomon's kingdom and the depths of the exile in Babylon. Read quickly through these chapters, and note in the table below what you learn in each category.

God's character e.g. Neh 9:17	
God's promises (covenants) e.g. Neh 9:8	
God's actions for Israel e.g. Neh 9:9-12	
Israel's sins e.g. Neh 9:26	
Israel's promises (covenants) e.g. Neh 9:38, 10:30	

- Daniel 9:3

- Jonah 3:1-5

- Matt 11:20-21

Optional: Mixing with foreigners

- Read Deuteronomy 7:1-6. Why was it was so important for the Israelites to keep themselves separate from the other nations?

- Read 1 Kings 11:1-13. What happened when Solomon disobeyed this commandment from God?

5. From Nehemiah 9:20 and 30, why did God give his Spirit?

6. Nehemiah 9:28 acts like a refrain for Israel, or a summary of the pattern of their relationship with God. How does this make you feel about the future of Israel after Nehemiah's reforms?

7. From each of the following passages, what significant issues are involved in Israel's new "firm covenant" with God?

- 10:29

- 10:30

- 10:31

- 10:32-39

Promises, promises

WITH DEEP AND GENUINE CONVICTION, Israel signed off on an agreement to once again keep the Law of Moses. Remember that way back in Deuteronomy, Moses had said this would be the sign of true, 'heart and soul' repentance. As we saw in question 7 above, the people of Israel earnestly promised to:

- separate themselves from other nations
- refuse to take foreign wives (the very thing that had brought Solomon undone)

- keep the Sabbath
- not trade greedily on the Lord's Day.

They even covenanted to reinstate all of the Levitical feasts, offerings, tithes and firstfruit sacrifices. Priests, servants, wives, sons and daughters: they all promised not to neglect the house of their God (10:39).

The covenant has been signed and sealed—but will it be delivered?

Before we find out (in the next study), there is a little more 'moving house' that must take place.

Quickly read Nehemiah 11–12:26.

8. Most of the Israelites are still living in villages outside the newly completed walls of Jerusalem. Why is it important that people live in Jerusalem (7:3-4, 11:19)?

9. What attitude do people have to those who settle in the city (11:1-2)?

10. What activities are the priests and Levites responsible for (12:1-26)?

THE LIST OF JEWS IN CHAPTERS 11-12, within and without Jerusalem, spans across many generations of returning exiles. It pulls together God's people in a way that goes beyond history. It unites them in their efforts to serve God, but also in their efforts to oppose the enemies of God.

It can seem to us a little futile to read long lists of names from millennia past. What possible value can it have for a servant of Jesus today? But these are not just lists of names—they fit into a story, the narrative of what God is doing in the world and how he can always be depended on to love individuals, to keep his promises to them, and to care whether or not they obey his word as their creator. It doesn't matter whether you are Bakbukiah the Levite or Bob Smith the plumber—you have a place in God's story.

But does God have a place in yours?

» Implications

(Choose one or more of the following to think about further or to discuss in your group.)

- In the Old Testament, God gave the people of Israel "saviours" (9:27) to rescue them from their enemies. In Jesus, people are saved from "the curse of the law" (Gal 3:13). Read Galatians 3:10-14 and then answer the following questions:

    - How was the law a curse on Israel?

- What is it that law-keeping could never achieve for Israel?

- Who benefits from Jesus' death, in which he became a curse for us?

- What are these benefits?

- God never gives up on his people, despite their repeated unfaithfulness to him. Does knowing this help you to avoid sin? Why/why not?

- Many people have no idea where they fit into the world. How can the story of God's covenant with Israel, and its fulfilment in Christ, help people to find direction in life?

- Read Luke 3:8-9. What practical steps can you take to put in place genuine repentance and commitment to living God's way? How can you protect yourself against slipping back into disobedience and not bearing good fruit?

» Give thanks and pray

- Remembering the mini history of God's people in Nehemiah 9, thank God for using Israel to help us understand the hopelessness of mankind, and the ultimate work of salvation on the cross.
- Thank God for sending Christ to redeem us from the curse of the law.
- Ask God's Spirit to help you persevere in reading God's word, and to help you resist the temptation to disobey God.

WHEN BACKS ARE TURNED

[NEHEMIAH 12:27-13:31]

1. Are you optimistic or pessimistic about your ability to remain firm in your faith and to resist temptations to sin? Why?

It was the best of times ...

> Like a dog that returns to his vomit
> is a fool who repeats his folly. (Prov 26:11)

THIS STRIKING PROVERB from the mind of Solomon could have been written for the Israelites we encounter in this closing section of Nehemiah.

To make matters worse, initially everything just seems so good. After the grand assembly recorded in Nehemiah 7:5-12:26, we return to the wall of Jerusalem, which is ready for dedication. A wonderful service of thanksgiving and praise is planned, with music to put even the most vibrant church to shame. A great sense of occasion develops, as the choirs of Israel move around the wall and towards the temple, rejoicing in God's goodness and his merciful restoration of their home city.

If only the last chapter of Nehemiah's diary need not have been written. As soon as Nehemiah's back is turned, the Israelites return to their old ways. And they do it in a flagrant and painful manner that is just too much for Nehemiah to bear.

But before we enter into his despair, let's enjoy the ceremony.

Optional: David

There is repeated mention of King David. Why? (Compare this occasion with the occasion and song recorded in 1 Chronicles 16:8-36.)

Read Nehemiah 12:27-13:3.

2. Summarize the ceremony that takes place in verses 27-43. What is it trying to achieve?

3. Think back to the written promises the people made and sealed in Nehemiah 10. From 12:44–13:3, do they seem to be keeping them?

... it was the worst of times

How could things go wrong at this point? Isn't this when the author finishes his diary with some platitudes and a godly flourish? Sadly, Nehemiah's memoirs follow the path of all biblical history—in and out of sin, and back into it again. Perhaps this is what makes it such a believable and accurate record of human endeavour and God's intervention. No-one would *invent* a national history that finished like this.

Read Nehemiah 13:4–31.

4. Which enemies of Israel have reappeared (vv. 4, 28; cf. Neh 2:10, 6:17-19)?

5. What does Eliashib do wrong?

6. The three promises made by all of Israel in Nehemiah 10 have each been breached. By referring to the verses, explain what the promise was, how it was broken, and who broke it.

Verses	Promise	How it was broken	Who broke it
10:30			
10:31			
10:39			

7. How does Nehemiah react to the sinning?

- Read verses 11, 17, 19, 21, 22, 25, 28 and 30, and then summarize his reaction.

- Would you say his reactions are justified?

8. List the measures Nehemiah puts in place to restore the keeping of the law (vv. 9, 12-13, 19, 22, 25-27, 30-31).

9. What is Nehemiah's opinion of Solomon?

10. Has there been any record in Nehemiah of sin on his part? What are we to make of this?

Judging Nehemiah

WE DON'T KNOW HOW LONG Nehemiah was away. After twelve years spent reconstructing Jerusalem, he kept his promise (Neh 2:6) to return to King Artaxerxes, who had given him leave in the first place. (Was ever there a man more of his word than Nehemiah?) But during his absence, things in Israel spiralled downwards. While Nehemiah's back was turned, Israel systematically reneged on the promises that it had signed and sealed as "a firm covenant in writing" (9:38). Nehemiah records their sins in distressing detail—we can almost feel his rage and frustration as he chronicles their failure.

But was Nehemiah himself a success or a failure? Did he achieve the task he set himself?

Let's return to a question from an earlier study. Consider Nehemiah's appeals to God in 13:14, 22 and 31. Having read the diary of Nehemiah, which of the following best paraphrases what Nehemiah seems to be praying here?

a) Reward me, God, because I have turned your people around.
b) Count up all my good deeds, God, because there are plenty of them.
c) I think I have done good deeds, God, even if everyone else has let you down.

Throughout the book, Nehemiah has been tossed back and forth between identifying with God's people, whom he loves and serves, and distancing himself from them when they sin and break covenant with God. Nehemiah is that rare biblical figure, the upright man, who perseveres in faithfulness while all around him descend into wickedness. In the end, his appeal to God seems to be more like (c), a prayer for mercy ("do not wipe out my good deeds"), than a claim to a reward.

Nehemiah despaired of Israel, and knew that judgement remained. For this reason, he asks that God will recognize his own acts of service and spare him in his steadfast love (13:22). On our side of the resurrection, we know that God did administer both his judgement and his love, when he spent his anger on his Son at the cross. He not only spared his upright servant, Nehemiah, but he even redeemed those who sinned under the first covenant, the Law of Moses (Heb 9:15).

There is far more hope for us than there was for Nehemiah as he scribed his memoirs, hoping to defend his time and deeds in the face of Israel's sin. We can see beyond these final pages of Old Testament history, on into the gospel age. We have even more reason to trust in the promises of God and the fulfilment of his plans to rebuild, renovate and revive his people.

Renovator's dream

In the end, the people of Israel do not turn back to God. More than that, they repeat the very sins of Solomon that sent them into exile in the past. What happened to 'heart and soul' repentance? They rebuilt the walls of Jerusalem, but ultimately they were not a rebuilt people. Their repentance proved to be only skin-deep. They were not a renovator's dream, but a renovator's nightmare.

Where will we find an Israel that meets God's requirements? And what will happen to the promise of God's restored blessing?

The answer, of course, is "in Christ". Christ himself is an 'Israel' that serves God completely—heart and soul. And through Christ, God's Spirit is at last made available. Now is the time of circumcised hearts that Moses (and Nehemiah) was longing for (Deut 30:6).

>> Implications

(Choose one or more of the following to think about further or to discuss in your group.)

- How do you react to sin?

  - Do you feel the same zeal for God that Nehemiah had?

  - In what ways would it be appropriate/inappropriate for us to respond to sin in the way Nehemiah did?

  - How do Jesus' words in Luke 6:41-42 help us to respond properly to sin?

- Does the command to be cleansed of everything foreign have any relevance to Christians today? Read Galatians 3:23-29 and 2 Corinthians 6:14-7:1 in shaping your answer.

- Read 1 John 1:1-6.

  - In what ways does this passage help us to understand the forgiveness that is ours in Christ, as well as the need to live holy and obedient lives?

  - Do you trust in Christ as your advocate before God, bringing forgiveness for sin?

  - Has God's Spirit moved you to love him by obeying his word?

» Give thanks and pray

- Thank God for sending Jesus to free us from the slavery of sin.
- Repent of your sins, begging forgiveness from God and asking him to help you to live a holy and obedient life.
- Ask God to give you a renewed urgency and passion to read and meditate on his word daily.

Feedback on this resource

We really appreciate getting feedback about our resources—not just suggestions for how to improve them, but also positive feedback and ways they can be used. We especially love to hear that the resources may have helped someone in their Christian growth.

You can send feedback to us via the 'Feedback' menu in our online store, or write to us at PO Box 225, Kingsford NSW 2032, Australia.

APPENDIX

»TIPS FOR LEADERS

Introductory notes for leaders

THE STUDIES IN *Renovator's Dream*, like all of the
Interactive and Topical Bible Studies from Matthias
Media, are designed to fall somewhere between a sermon
and a set of plain discussion questions. The idea is to provide a little more direction and information than you
would normally see in a set of printed Bible studies, but
to maintain an emphasis on personal investigation,
thought, discovery and application. We aim to give input
and help, without doing all the work for the
reader/studier.

If you're about to lead your group through these studies
on Nehemiah, get ready for a few surprises! The first surprise is that Nehemiah isn't nearly as dull as some people
in your group might be expecting. It's a first-person
account of determination and intrigue that could easily
have you and your group members sitting on the edge of
your seats.

The second surprise is that the contents of the book of
Nehemiah may differ from what people are expecting.
There is a long tradition of treating Nehemiah as the
Bible's 'leadership guru'—the Tom Peters or Stephen R
Covey of ancient Israel. But a careful reading of the text
will show that in spite of Nehemiah's pursuit of excellence,
and even though he adopted all seven habits of highly
effective leadership, this is a story of failure. The stony
walls of Israel were rebuilt, but the stony hearts of Israel
remained. The story may climax with a great celebration

of repentance, but it is followed by a dramatic anti-climax that leaves Nehemiah wringing his hands, and the reader wondering what sort of leader it will ultimately take to change the hearts of Israel.

So what tips will help you effectively lead your study group through Nehemiah? First and most importantly, please read the *whole* of Nehemiah in a single sitting before you start leading your group. Note Nehemiah's noble dream at the start of the book, and weigh up his progress as the story unfolds. Note the glorious threefold promises of obedience made by enthusiastic Israel, and then watch how the promises pan out.

Stephen R Covey says that highly effective leaders will always "begin with the end in mind". In the case of Nehemiah, that's great advice. Having the end in mind doesn't mean you don't enjoy the process of discovery. Your job as leader is to guide your group through this process over a number of weeks. Enjoy the perseverance of the builders, celebrate the good times along the way, but leave room for a note of incompletion and dissatisfaction. And feel the frustration at the end of the book that leaves you longing for something more.

Significantly, Nehemiah is the final book in the historical narratives of the Old Testament. It's important that, as group leader, you have a clear grasp of the fact that the whole Old Testament leads us to, and prepares us for, the coming of Jesus Christ. And what better way for the Old Testament story to close than with the story of a leader who almost made the grade, but who couldn't change hearts?

Phil Campbell and Greg Clarke

LIKE ALL OUR STUDIES, THESE are designed to work in a group on the assumption that the group members have worked through the material in advance. If this is not happening in your group, it will obviously change the way you lead the study.

If the group is preparing ...

If all is well, and the group is well prepared, then reading through *all* the text and answering *all* the questions will be time consuming and probably quite boring. These studies are not designed to work this way in a group.

The leader needs to go through the study thoroughly in advance and work out how to lead a group discussion using the text and questions as a basis. You should be able to follow the order of the study through pretty much as it is written. But you will need to work out which things you are going to omit, which you are going to glide over quite quickly, and which you are going to concentrate on and perhaps add supplementary discussion questions to.

Obviously, as with all studies, this process of selection and augmentation will be based on what your *aims* are for this study for your particular group. You need to work out where you want to get to as a main emphasis or teaching point or application point at the end. The material itself will certainly head you in a particular direction, but there will usually be various emphases you can bring out, and a variety of applications to think about.

The slabs of text need to be treated as a resource for discussion, not something to be simply read out. This will mean highlighting portions to talk about, adding supplementary discussion questions and ideas to provoke discussion where you think that would be helpful for your particular group, and so on.

The same is true for the Bible study and 'Implications' questions. You need to be selective, according to where you want the whole thing to go. Some questions you will want to do fairly quickly or omit altogether. Others you will want to concentrate on—because they are difficult or because they are crucial or both—and in these cases you may want to add a few questions of your own if you think it would help.

You may also need to add some probing questions of your own if your group is giving too many 'pat' answers, or just reproducing the ideas in the text sections without actually grappling with the biblical text for themselves.

There is room for flexibility. Some groups, for example, read the text and do the Bible study questions in advance, but save the 'Implications' questions for the group discussion.

If the group isn't preparing ...

This obviously makes the whole thing a lot harder (as with any study). Most of the above still applies. But if your group is not doing much preparation, your role is even more crucial and active. You will have to be even more careful in your selection and emphasis and supplementary questions—you will have to convey the basic content, as well as develop it in the direction of personal application. Reading through the *whole* study in the group will still be hard going. In your selection, you will probably need to read more sections of text together (selecting the important bits), and will not be able to glide over comprehension questions so easily.

If the group is not preparing, it does make it harder—not impossible, but a good reason for encouraging your group to do at least some preparation.

Conclusion

No set of printed studies can guarantee a good group learning experience. No book can take the place of a well-prepared thoughtful leader who knows where he or she wants to take the group, and guides them gently along that path.

Our Bible studies aim to be a resource and handbook for that process. They will do a lot of the work for you. All the same, they need to be *used* not simply followed.

Tony Payne
Series Editor

matthiasmedia

Matthias Media is an evangelical publishing ministry that seeks to persuade all Christians of the truth of God's purposes in Jesus Christ as revealed in the Bible, and equip them with high-quality resources, so that by the work of the Holy Spirit they will:

- abandon their lives to the honour and service of Christ in daily holiness and decision-making
- pray constantly in Christ's name for the fruitfulness and growth of his gospel
- speak the Bible's life-changing word whenever and however they can— in the home, in the world and in the fellowship of his people.

It was in 1988 that we first started pursuing this mission, and in God's kindness we now have more than 300 different ministry resources being used all over the world. These resources range from Bible studies and books through to training courses and audio sermons.

To find out more about our large range of very useful resources, and to access samples and free downloads, visit our website:

www.matthiasmedia.com.au

How to buy our resources

1. Direct from us over the internet:
   - in the US: www.matthiasmedia.com
   - in Australia and the rest of the world: www.matthiasmedia.com.au

2. Direct from us by phone:
   - in the US: 1 866 407 4530
   - in Australia: 1800 814 360 (Sydney: 9663 1478)
   - international: +61-2-9663-1478

> Register at our website for our **free** regular email update to receive information about the latest new resources, **exclusive special offers**, and free articles to help you grow in your Christian life and ministry.

3. Through a range of outlets in various parts of the world. Visit **www.matthiasmedia.com.au/information/contact-us** for details about recommended retailers in your part of the world, including www.thegoodbook.co.uk in the United Kingdom.

4. Trade enquiries can be addressed to:
   - in the US and Canada: sales@matthiasmedia.com
   - in Australia and the rest of the world: sales@matthiasmedia.com.au

Other Interactive and Topical Bible Studies from Matthias Media

Our Interactive Bible Studies (IBS) and Topical Bible Studies (TBS) are a valuable resource to help you keep feeding from God's word. The IBS series works through passages and books of the Bible; the TBS series pulls together the Bible's teaching on topics such as money or prayer. As at January 2011, the series contains the following titles:

Beyond Eden
GENESIS 1-11
Authors: Phillip Jensen and
Tony Payne, 9 studies

Out of Darkness
EXODUS 1-18
Author: Andrew Reid, 8 studies

The Shadow of Glory
EXODUS 19-40
Author: Andrew Reid, 7 studies

The One and Only
DEUTERONOMY
Author: Bryson Smith, 8 studies

The Good, the Bad and the Ugly
JUDGES
Author: Mark Baddeley,
10 studies

Famine and Fortune
RUTH
Authors: Barry Webb and
David Höhne, 4 studies

Renovator's Dream
NEHEMIAH
Authors: Phil Campbell and
Greg Clarke, 7 studies

The Eye of the Storm
JOB
Author: Bryson Smith, 6 studies

The Beginning of Wisdom
PROVERBS VOLUME 1
Author: Joshua Ng, 7 studies

The Search for Meaning
ECCLESIASTES
Author: Tim McMahon, 9 studies

Two Cities
ISAIAH
Authors: Andrew Reid and
Karen Morris, 9 studies

Kingdom of Dreams
DANIEL
Authors: Andrew Reid and
Karen Morris, 9 studies

Burning Desire
OBADIAH AND MALACHI
Authors: Phillip Jensen and
Richard Pulley, 6 studies

Warning Signs
JONAH
Author: Andrew Reid, 6 studies

On That Day
ZECHARIAH
Author: Tim McMahon, 8 studies

Full of Promise
THE BIG PICTURE OF THE O.T.
Authors: Phil Campbell
and Bryson Smith, 8 studies

The Good Living Guide
MATTHEW 5:1-12
Authors: Phillip Jensen and
Tony Payne, 9 studies

News of the Hour
MARK
Authors: Peter Bolt and Tony
Payne, 10 studies

Proclaiming the Risen Lord
LUKE 24-ACTS 2
Author: Peter Bolt, 6 studies

Mission Unstoppable
ACTS
Author: Bryson Smith, 10 studies

The Free Gift of Life
ROMANS 1-5
Author: Gordon Cheng, 8 studies

The Free Gift of Sonship
ROMANS 6-11
Author: Gordon Cheng, 8 studies

The Freedom of Christian Living
ROMANS 12-16
Author: Gordon Cheng, 7 studies

Free for All
GALATIANS
Authors: Phillip Jensen
and Kel Richards, 8 studies

Walk this Way
EPHESIANS
Author: Bryson Smith, 8 studies

Partners for Life
PHILIPPIANS
Author: Tim Thorburn, 8 studies

The Complete Christian
COLOSSIANS
Authors: Phillip Jensen and
Tony Payne, 8 studies

To the Householder
1 TIMOTHY
Authors: Phillip Jensen and
Greg Clarke, 9 studies

Run the Race
2 TIMOTHY
Author: Bryson Smith, 6 studies

The Path to Godliness
TITUS
Authors: Phillip Jensen and
Tony Payne, 7 studies

From Shadow to Reality
HEBREWS
Author: Joshua Ng, 10 studies

The Implanted Word
JAMES
Authors: Phillip Jensen and
Kirsten Birkett, 8 studies

Homeward Bound
1 PETER
Authors: Phillip Jensen and
Tony Payne, 10 studies

All You Need to Know
2 PETER
Author: Bryson Smith, 6 studies

The Vision Statement
REVELATION
Author: Greg Clarke, 9 studies

Bold I Approach
PRAYER
Author: Tony Payne, 6 studies

Cash Values
MONEY
Author: Tony Payne, 5 studies

Sing for Joy
SINGING IN CHURCH
Author: Nathan Lovell, 6 studies

The Blueprint
DOCTRINE
Authors: Phillip Jensen and
Tony Payne, 9 studies

Woman of God
THE BIBLE ON WOMEN
Author: Terry Blowes, 8 studies